UNDERSTANDING AND
MENDING BROKEN PATHS

UNDERSTANDING AND MENDING BROKEN PATHS

UNDERSTANDING AND MENDING BROKEN PATHS

SEAN ALEXANDER HAMILTON

UNDERSTANDING AND MENDING BROKEN PATHS

For information contact:
www.alexanderhamiltonsinsights.com

Editor: Alyssa Asaro
Line Editor: Ray-Anne Lutener
Cover Designer: Olga Vynnychenko
Image credit: Aimee Vogelsang on Unsplash.

Dedication

I'd like to dedicate this to everyone along the path to understanding.

CONTENTS

Acknowledgments

I want to thank all the people that have come into my life during my brokenness and helped me understand it.

I also want to thank my mentor, Sky Benson, for helping me with the title creation.

Lastly, I want to thank my editor Alyssa Asaro who, through her editing skills, has helped me make this book a masterpiece.

Introduction

As we walk along the road of life, we enjoy good times and capture treasured memories that we hold dear to our hearts. We also face adversity when ugly and more negative experiences appear as broken cracks in the pavement, diverting us from the path we had chosen.

You may have thought to yourself, "How can I get off this path and go in a completely new direction?"

If you have ever watched a movie or read a book based on a true story, where the person had to get over some sort of broken and tragic ordeal, then you know how we can relate our life experiences to those of others.

I know these types of stories have shed light and acknowledgement on my own broken paths, and I imagine that they have done the same for you.

Try to remember that we're all on a path whether that's a positive or a negative one.

In one way or another, we all have similar stories. Just because someone is smiling and laughing doesn't mean they're not living with a broken heart or trying to move on from negative experiences in their lives.

This book is about getting to the heart of your broken path so that you can move onto a path of self-healing, self-discovery, self-understanding and freedom. As you read through the pages of this book, I will be right there with you as a guide.

Let's embark on understanding this journey together.

> *"Something that is broken can*
>
> *be put back together again*
>
> *piece by piece."*

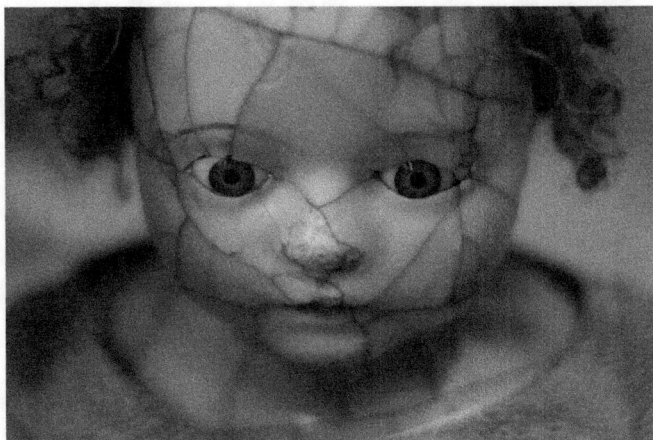

Sean Alexander Hamilton

Chapter One

BROKEN PIECES

AS WE WALK along those broken paths in life, we shall encounter negative transformative experiences and situations, that will either make us or break us.

They can shape our lives in ways we didn't think were possible and will change the course that we're on.

These negative experiences and situations can follow us like broken, fractured shadows and continue to plague our daily lives long after the actual event.

These broken fragments of our life come in different forms of emotional experience from different stages in our life. I can't be certain when you will experience them, but

I can tell you this. The walk seems to be long and lonely along the cracked path you find yourself on, but you're not alone and you don't have to be scared.

These shattering experiences will ultimately form the basis of who you will become. They will give you purpose, meaning and determine your direction of travel.

It's important that we focus on this positive mindset, so we don't take the wrong turn in life and stay trapped under the weight of the pain of these broken moments.

I know that moments in my past have affected my own current state, which is why I feel able to speak about them so freely.

We have to identify what specific emotional experiences have caused us to shut down and make a change for either the better or for the worse.

We should make notes of the emotional states we're in and the timeline of when we noticed them taking place. Then we should reflect on those feelings.

Once we can figure out which feelings are associated with the negative past experiences, then we can start to rebuild our emotional and mental resilience and make ourselves whole again, ready for our new journey to begin. This new journey is one of much-needed self-discovery and self-healing. We don't want to stay haunted with the emotional nightmare of our negative experiences.

I speak of this because I have been there on my personal journey. Once I became aware of these moments and accepted enlightenment, I started to become more aware of the same emotional traits in other people.

I began to wonder how we move onto a different path than the one we started on. When I compared my own broken emotional responses to past experiences and situations with those in other people that encountered, I realized the stages were all similar.

So, let's move onto the stages of brokenness.

We should understand these stages in order to break free from the broken emotional responses that have such a strong hold on us.

How do we acknowledge the challenge if we don't understand the stages of the brokenness?

Each stage will affect us differently and each stage will move us away from what I believe to be the ultimate goal in one's life, which is to live in harmony with any emotional response we carry throughout our lives.

"BROKENNESS IS OFTEN THE ROAD TO BREAKTHROUGH. BE ENCOURAGED"

Tony Evana

NOTES

NOTES

_____

_____

_____

_____

_____

_____

_____

_____

_____

_____

_____

_____

NOTES

_____

_____

_____

_____

_____

_____

_____

_____

_____

_____

_____

_____

_____

Chapter Two

STAGES OF BROKENNESS

NOW WE GET INTO THE HEART OF WHY WE HAVE COME TO FEEL SO BROKEN.

On many occasions, our negative emotional responses (NER) in life can be traced back to specific transformational experiences and situations.

Most of you know exactly what I'm talking about and you have a clear understanding of the experiences that are at the core of your current mindset.

It can be useful to consider these events as stages on your personal journey along the broken path, or paths, life has led you down.

A specific event or stage will affect you not only on different emotional levels but also at different times on your journey.

Your personal path is unique, but there are some common threads that bind us to the universal pattern in everyone's life.

Recognizing that there are common events and experiences that unite us is a positive step in the right direction but being able to accept them is sometimes hard to do. Especially when you don't want to deal with the profound negative emotions associated with them.

So many of us don't have the mental energy to carry the weight of these negative past life experiences and we go into a state of denial and remission as a form of self-protection.

Recognizing Negative Experiences

Every negative event or stage has its own inherent degree of impact on our emotional state, which can be separate from the underlining problem, issue, or cause.

The stages can be brought about by sudden tragic events, or a lot of the time they can seem to come out of nowhere.

One thing is common, however: the deep negative emotional response we suffer is the same.

The only way to truly understand these stages is to have lived through them.

In this chapter I want to discuss two life experiences in depth: **Loss and Loneliness**.

LOSS

Most people have lost something or lost someone on their journey through life.

This experience brings about the deep emotional responses of sorrow, sadness, emptiness, fear, and loneliness.

The feeling of loss can arise from numerous events and situations in your life.

For example, **losing a job** is one of the simplest ways to understand how loss can bring about a deep and very negative emotional response.

What happens when we face the prospect of losing our job, perhaps during a lay off or even being fired? Emptiness and fear set in.

The negative response of emptiness is particularly painful when you associate your identity with your job and suddenly you are out of work.

Then fear of the unknown sets in because of the uncertainty and not knowing what will happen, financially and personally going forward.

Another example of loss comes from a sudden break-up in a marriage or relationship.

We respond with repressed anger, fear, and possibly resentment which makes it very difficult to move on.

When we invest deep emotional energy, time and effort into staying in a relationship with someone and it doesn't end the way we thought it would, so many of us become bitter.

This bitterness builds into a limiting belief which blocks us from even trying to start over and getting to know someone new.

We think "what is the point if we're going to end up most likely with the same outcome as before?"

This kind of limiting belief is a form of self-protection which has evolved to prevent us from feeling the deep pain of rejection and fear again. But it can make it very hard for the heart to move forward and open up to a new relationship without experiencing worry, concern, and trust issues.

Another example of losing someone is probably the hardest experience to go through depending on whom you ask.

This is the loss of a loved one.

We can lose someone we love deeply as a result of, for example, a tragic health problem, a car accident, old age, murder, or suicide.

The emotional experience of such deep loss holds so many intricate parts to it, that it can take years to free yourself from a very real but understandable state of depression following the loss of the loved one.

Following the loss, your mental state can feel like a constant emotional roller coaster. Conflicting emotions rush over you and they can be so difficult to deal with that it is hard to see a way forward.

Once technique is to focus on more positive recollections of the happy times that we spent with the loved ones we have lost. Those warm memories of laughter, love, embraces, and caring moments can help with this stage.

LONELINESS

For many, loneliness is one of the most demanding, darkest and negative emotional experiences. The longer this stage persists, the more the sufferer can feel totally lost and unable to see a light at the end of the tunnel.

To the outside world a deeply lonely person may appear totally normal and content, but this hides a range of destructive and negative feelings that are raging on the inside.

If you look close enough you can often see signs of someone's loneliness and inner despair in subtle changes in their outward appearance such as their posture and facial expressions to voice fluctuations.

Internally, loneliness can make you feel very lost with no one to save you from the void of emptiness and complete loss of intimacy and companionship.

We don't want to lose our way in this dark place on a broken pathway we call loneliness. But we can very well slip into the void on either side of the path and feel as though nothing will, or can, pull us out.

This world might feel desperately lonely when everyone around us seems to be caught up in their own self-contained daily lives and as you walk down the street all you hear are your own footsteps.

Even when you walk along the shoreline on the beach, all you notice when you turn around are your own footprints in the sand.

When we start feeling this type of emotional response to our situation, we need to look ahead and see the other footprints in the sand in front of us.

Those footsteps were made by other people just like us. Everyone has experienced loneliness in their life at one time or another and maybe, just maybe, this is just one more transient stage on life's turbulent pathway.

It's at this point we should start to see the lighter part of the path ahead and feel some calmness in our heart knowing that loneliness is only created in our mind and that we're never truly alone.

NOTES

NOTES

Chapter Three

REFLECTIONS ALONG THE PATH

Aristotle once said that wisdom (the ability to make good decisions) is a combination of experience plus reflection. The more time that you take to think about your experiences, the more vital lessons you will gain from them.

Brian Tracy

THE REFLECTIONS ALONG THE PATH are the memories of negative experiences and situations that we reflect on the most in our current life.

The question is: which memories and experiences do you want to reflect on the most? Believe it or not there are only two real options when it comes to this.

OPTION ONE

is the one we usually default to. Our Negative Emotional Responses (NER).

Focusing on and revisiting these negative transformational experiences over and over again can be detrimental in developing who we truly want to become.

Reflecting on these painful moments and experiences from the past can effectively block our ability to create new significant relationships and develop meaningful insights about ourselves.

In addition, the three "Rs" which are part of our new path will be impacted: **Revision. Rebuilding. Restoring.**

These are the essential tools to help us get an understanding of the one person we should understand the most.

As not to get off topic, let's continue and we will revisit these three Rs in a later chapter.

OPTION TWO

is the far better alternative and I'm hoping this one takes hold of you and overshadows the first option.

It's Positive Emotional Responses (PER).

What this can do for you is help with the three Rs and makes them most effective in reshaping your life.

We can live <u>under the shadow</u> of our painful pasts experiences or we can live <u>within the lessons</u> we have learnt from these painful moments.

We can all recognize that certain memories and events will trigger an emotional response and take us back to that moment.

Reflections on our past experiences and situations will always come in and out of our life. There is no stopping them. They are part of the path that we're on.

It's how we chose to respond to these emotional triggers that will define who we are and how close we are to changing any present event.

Negative Emotional Responses or Positive Emotional Responses?

The road to understanding is sometimes a difficult path to take, especially when things seem so broken in our current life. But thank God that we have these moments of connection and reflection because they give us the clarity and foresight to change our path and begin stepping onto a new one.

If I were to give you two separate ways to make it to your destination in life, which one would you choose?

Say for instance you have already taken one of those two paths. But it didn't work out the way you thought it was going too and you didn't get the outcome that you wanted.

Now ask yourself. Would you take the same path you have just been on, or would you choose the other untested path?

It's at this point is when we need to focus and take the time to reflect on what has transpired over the course of past years.

Sometimes we answer the call for change with self-doubt and fear that the other untested path will end the same way.

So, we take the same familiar path because we already know what to expect.

This is always not the best course of action. Whatever compels us to do this I don't know. Perhaps it is fear of the unknown?

But what I do know is this. Whichever path we choose to take, change will follow as a result. Will it be based on **Negative Emotional Responses or Positive Emotional Responses?**

That's why we should pay close attention to what we chose to reflect on.

We have to think about our responses to emotional triggers and the feelings we have attached to those responses.

Now I'm not telling you not to take another attempt at a relationship. But what I am saying if it continues to not go the way you planned, then at some point we have to take the hard decision to move onto the other path to get a different result.

The definition of insanity, as Albert Einstein once said,

"... is doing the same thing over and over again and expecting different results."

When this happens, we must be able to forgive ourselves for being wrong. There is nothing wrong with this at all; fear of the unknown is not a weakness, it is natural and only makes us human.

You will find that taking time to reflect on how we respond to emotional triggers brings seeds of understanding, acknowledgment, and forethought.

Let's dive into this in the next chapter, and the next level of understanding along your path.

NOTES

_____

_____

_____

_____

_____

_____

_____

_____

_____

_____

_____

_____

NOTES

Chapter Four

PATHWAYS TO FREEDOM

HOW DO WE FREE OURSELVES of being trapped in a cycle of negative emotional responses?

Well, forgiveness is a good place to start. Let's explore how forgiveness is one important step on your new pathway to freedom.

Forgiveness

What does the term forgiveness truly mean?

Well the Webster definition is "to give up resentment or claim to requital for (an offense or wrong); pardon."

Understanding the true impact of forgiveness is the first key to unlocking the door to personal freedom.

Each stage on the pathway to freedom through forgiveness can be broken down into smaller steps.

Starting with the most fundamental and essential step of all.

The very first person you should forgive is always yourself.

Forgiving yourself gives you the power to:

- understand yourself on a deeper level
- forgive yourself for past events and situations that were completely out of your control.

It is all too easy to blame ourselves for negative events that were caused by the actions of other people and, as a result, were totally out of our control.

We need to keep reminding ourselves of this as we continue on the way towards freedom.

Until we forgive the one person we should have forgiven at the start – ourselves- then we cannot move on to forgive the actions of others, and the outcomes of those actions.

Unless we take the step of personal self-forgiveness, we will stay locked in a cycle of NER in every situation.

Turning these negative emotional responses into bitterness is one of the most destructive courses we can take.

So, we must stop this before it happens.

How do you do this?

Well forgiveness is the first step and there are bound to be a multitude of events, decisions and actions that we should forgive ourselves for.

<u>Example One.</u> A loved one passing away and going to the other side, whatever the "other side" means for you (heaven, reincarnation, another dimension, or the other side).

I know that when this happens, we can feel responsible and punish ourselves in the mistaken belief that we could have done something, or should have done more, to keep them here with us.

The truth of the matter is, as much as we cared about our loved ones, we could not foresee their passing. This is just one more moment or situation in life that was out of our control.

So, we must forgive ourselves for this tragic loss that we were powerless to prevent.

There is nobody to blame.

Because if we do shift the blame onto ourselves, we will feel lost, lonely, and helpless.

This will take us even further away from the pathway to freedom.

Example Two. Another example of a moment that you can't control is someone getting up and walking out of your relationship.

We also tend to start blaming ourselves for this type of loss and immediately start to question what happened.

What went wrong between us?

Or, was there something I could have done to fix it?

It's absolutely okay to have these questions. In fact, it is normal, because you cared about this person.

These questions can take you into two different directions of thought.

They could lead you into despair and despondency or they could lead you into deeper clarity and understanding.

Clarity is what we want in order to reach the pathway of freedom.

Making sense of it all, then moving into the realm of understanding is what we want to do.

In order to do this, I wrote down a personal pathway to freedom that I will now share with you.

From my personal journal

NOTE TO SELF

In time, love will give way to forgiveness.

Forgiveness will then guide you through the darkness and out into the light of just being.

The soul will enter the realm of enlightenment.

Finding truth that it seeks not through our soulmate but within the very soul that we hold inside of ourselves.

For time can only heal the broken pieces we hide from others.

Why must we hold onto these attachments of pain, sorrow, hurt, and loneliness?

Is there a way back to the place we left our true selves behind?

In the shadows of love lives the fear that love is not in this lifetime or even in the next.

Love holds a place inside of us that we all long for.

We find this love through happiness.

So, I have come to the conclusion that happiness brings love, and love doesn't bring happiness.

This type of inner love will break down the barriers we have created within ourselves.

But only the equation of H+L=IL Happiness plus Love equals Inner Love can bring me back to me.

The love you offer to a soulmate is different from the love you should feel for yourself.

The more I love you, the more I distance myself from you because it is not in this love where you find peace but only in the happiness of love you offer to yourself.

I tell you this with an open heart of understanding that to be with you is to not be with you.

I don't expect you to understand but I do hope one day that once this type of love is found within your soul, the question will be answered.

My love for you can release me from this imprisonment I have only created myself.

For you're the only one who holds the key to the treasure that's inside of you.

Until then it shall remain locked, waiting ever so patiently for your return home.

Remember my love isn't the key it is only the mystical, magical, and mysterious equation (H+L= I L) of the spell you have me under that can **SET ME FREE!**

Once this is done you will also be set free from the attachments that keep you from me, and ultimately keep you from yourself.

PLEASE I AM HERE AND I

AM WAITING.

This is something I wrote to remind myself that it was about time that I worked on attaining my goal of personal freedom.

So far, it has helped me tremendously in giving me direction.

You never want to be in limbo, worrying and uncertain, burning with lots of unanswered questions.

This is called the closure phase.

The closure phase brings you to the stage of being reborn and finding yourself again.

So, getting closure in this way is part of the pathway to your newfound freedom.

Without closure, moving towards a new beginning is difficult to do.

So, we must complete this closure phase.

When we have closure, we have clarity of thought and motion.

If the mind is filled with all the clutter of negative thoughts and events, it makes it hard to move on to better things and new beginnings.

This is a very important step in being able to move away from where you are now to where you are meant to be.

Clear thoughts, vision, and movement help us to reach this closure phase.

Now I will briefly go over the three Rs.

Revision

Revision is the act of looking at things with a new set of eyes.

We should view our path not through a cracked lens but with hope and a sense of resurgence.

For this we must look into ourselves and know that this path won't be broken forever.

This will give us strength to begin the challenging process of restoring and rebuilding.

Restoring

Restoring is the act of putting something back together.

The first thing that should be put back together is the way we think about ourselves. We're the direct reflection of how we see ourselves.

We need to have a positive inner dialogue with ourselves in order to start the restoration process.

You must remember that you're the most important person in your life.

Having a negative dialogue with yourself could translate into responding negatively towards others which in turn will delay your own healing process.

Rebuilding

Rebuilding is the intentional act of building upwards with new levels.

The deliberate act of rebuilding can be directed in all areas of our lives, such as rebuilding a house that has been torn down, rebuilding your bank account after financial losses, and rebuilding your relationship with your significant other.

But what I'm most interested in, and what this book is mainly about, is rebuilding your relationship with yourself.

How do we do this? By reconnecting with the very foundation of who we are. Just like when rebuilding a house, you must have a strong foundation so it can withstand the reoccurring negative experiences and situations that threaten us.

"Don't allow your wounds to transform you into someone you are not"

Paulo Coelho

NOTES

Chapter Five

HEALING FOOTSTEPS ON HEALING STONES

EVERY BROKEN CRACK IN THE ROAD can be repaired with healing footsteps on healing stones.

I'm not talking about the crystalized stones that you find at new age stores.

I'm talking about the positive emotional responses that we have when negative events happen in or lives.

I know that you must be thinking - here we go again with the positive mental attitude (PMA) stuff.

I'm going to explain why this PER concept is much more important than the PMA concept first, because it's such an important part of the healing process.

Both concepts are similar in nature, but one holds more tangible power than the other.

Let's start off by defining the PMA concept for those of us that don't know.

Positive Mental Attitude Concept

This concept was first developed and introduced back in 1937 by Napoleon Hill in the book *Think and Grow Rich*.

The book never actually uses the term, but it develops the importance of positive thinking as a principle to success.

Napoleon Hill along with W. Clement Stone later wrote *Success Through A Positive*

Mental Attitude which defines positive mental attitude as comprising "the plus" characteristics symbolized by such words as faith, integrity, hope, optimism, courage, initiative, generosity, tolerance, tact, kindness, and common sense.

Positive mental attitude is the philosophy that having an optimistic disposition in every situation attracts positive change and increases achievement.

Adherents employ a state of mind that continue to seek, find, and execute ways to win or find a desirable outcome regardless of the circumstances.

Because of its fundamental nature, a positive mental attitude naturally opposes negativity, defeatism, and hopelessness.

Optimism and hope are vital to the development of PMA.

This concept is important because the thoughts we hold in our heads are what trigger certain responses.

The most influential people have said through the ages "how you think, is how you'll become"!

Buddha. Jesus Christ.

"Healing doesn't mean the damage never existed, it means the damage no longer controls our lives"

Anonymous

Now the concept that follows is what matters the most and is the **Positive Emotional Response Concept (PER).**

If we could train our minds to only think with a positive mental attitude, then by default the effects would be positive.

But what I have found is that we as humans separate these two concepts and think that they either don't follow the same guidelines or the same laws.

While this may be true, it's the connection and synergy between the two ideas that makes them work.

To make these positive emotional responses work for us, we have to understand both concepts and how we can use them to facilitate growth and personal development.

Positive Emotional Response Concept

The positive emotional response concept comes into play when thinking about a decision that has already been made, or an action that has already been taken.

We have to decide whether we have a positive or negative emotional response to this experience or situation.

Will we decide to focus on and think only about the negativity in our lives?

Will we allow ourselves to let in defeat, anger, sadness, worry, rejection, or hopelessness?

Or will we think positively in the way of redemption, revival, reshaping, and resurgence.

Every choice has the potential to lead us to healing footsteps on healing stones.

By choosing to stay negative, we will continue to walk along broken paths over and over again that are ultimately lonely and destructive.

How many people do you know who have gone back to old habits?

This person felt trapped whether they were in a bad relationship, or had an addiction (to alcohol, hard drugs, gambling, etc.).

They saw no way out, so they defaulted back to the old ways.

It's okay to be on a broken path.

But please remember not to lose yourself and your sense of direction on it.

We want to find the healing stones or otherwise healing moments and walk upon those stones instead of broken slabs.

These healing stones will present themselves to you, if you listen closely to your thoughts then respond to them positively.

It's the response that matters in the end.

That's why it's the most important part of the healing process.

Thoughts are just a preview to what response we take.

If we can change our mindset then we'll reach a better solution to our brokenness.

- Choose on a direction of thought.

- Decide on an outcome.

- Act upon the solution to get there.

So be accepting of the healing stones that have been placed in front of each step you take along your broken path.

It could be a person in your life, it could be a song that changes you from the inside, and it could be this book.

But whatever it is, accept it and embrace it for all it's worth because you're worth it.

"HEALING comes when we CHOOSE to walk away from darkness and move towards a Brighter Light."

Dieter F. Uchtdorf

NOTES

NOTES

"Possess the right thinking

only then can one receive the

gift of knowledge, strength,

and peace."

Master Splinter

Chapter Six

YOU'RE NOT ALONE ON THIS PATH

SO MANY OF US THINK we're completely alone on this path because of the brokenness and pain we have been through.

We feel that no one knows or can understand what we're going through.

Not true.

If we just look around us will see that many people have been broken by challenging experiences such as a breakup, loss of a loved one, divorce, or the end of a friendship.

These are all experiences and situations that tear at our hearts and depending who you ask, what mental state they're in, and how recent the brokenness has occurred, we sometimes might not understand how alone they really are.

If you listen closely you might catch a glimpse of what they are feeling at that moment.

Do your best to be there for one another and don't shift blame to the other person for either not letting you in, or not responding quickly enough to the heartache you have just told them about.

The loneliest journey or path is one we choose to go on alone.

Some of you may ask yourself what the loneliest journey is.

For a lot of people, it's being single without anyone to talk to!

Now, there are three types of single people out there so let's examine each of them.

First. Is the person who chooses to be single by default because they don't want to get hurt again.

This journey for them can be quite challenging as they become very introspective. They are always questioning their self-worth!

Questions they ask themselves are:

- What is wrong with me?

- Why can't I get past the hurt, anger, and resentment that I feel?

Strangely, we seem to want to hold onto negative feelings about previous relationships because we're not ready to let the other person go. Even if we feel bad at least we still have a connection to them in our mind.

Well I got some great news for this person. There is hope!

This is the journey of self-examination and rediscovery for you.

This is the time to reclaim your life back and let go of feelings of loss and betrayal.

It's time to let your previous love go, so that you can know what it truly means to love yourself again. Only then will you be ready to look for a new relationship with someone who will value you for who you truly are.

But if this isn't accomplished, you just might stay single.

So, reclaim that part of your life back and open up your mind and broken heart again to the simple idea of happiness and love from another person.

Let go of the feelings of hurt and the limiting belief that everyone is the same.

Move away from your Negative Emotional Response (NER) when meeting someone new or starting a new relationship.

Everyone is different and everyone has been through his or her own unique experiences of brokenness.

Remember one thing: you're not alone on what can feel like the loneliest journey of your life!

Forgive yourself and don't over analyze where you might have gone wrong or what you could have done differently to prevent what happened in your previous relationship or relationships.

The truth of the matter is, you couldn't have done anything differently because that moment is gone. It's in the past and you can't change a thing.

This moment, right now, however, is yours.

You can do things differently. You may not be able to change the actions of others towards you, but you can decide how you view them and respond to them.

Let go, in order to move forward.

By moving forward, we move onto a better life which is where your freedom journey truly begins.

In this exact moment we become stronger!

Until we do this, we still hold onto the weakness that comes with the question of why?

To build strength, we need to think about how to get past the weakness that stems from our negative experiences, situations and tragic events.

Strength comes from the answer.

Remember one thing. Even through your loneliest journey, you're not alone.

So, rise with understanding and reclaim what is rightfully yours.

Cut yourself from the pain others gave you, so you can give yourself the happiness you truly deserve.

The beautiful thing about this emergence is you leave room from another person to fill the void that someone else left.

---

*"IT HURTS THE MOST
WHEN THE PERSON THAT
MADE YOU FEEL SPECIAL
YESTERDAY MAKES YOU
FEEL SO UNWANTED TODAY"*

Now the second type of single person is someone who isn't single but feels that they are alone.

I believe that this is one of the hardest types of loneliness to face.

You might feel hopeless and useless in this situation.

It's hard to break free from this phase, because even though you're not really single, you're emotionally single and that's just terrible.

Feeling trapped, you stay in a loveless and unhappy relationship, where you feel isolated and crippled by the fear of not knowing how to get out.

But you're not alone, no matter how lonely your journey may seem, and there is hope.

The two sides of this hope have a negative draw back and a positive forward movement.

The negative drawback is staying in the relationship in the hope that the other person will change. We will stay on this lonely pathway through sadness and heartache day and night in the hope that our relationship will get better.

The sad reality is that we would rather settle rather than face being alone.

This might seem like a positive emotional response, but it isn't.

This usually happens when you have little ones to take care of, which is very understandable to a certain extent.

Once children become a part of the equation, we must take a step backwards and ask ourselves "if my child was going through this what would I tell them?"

If the answer is that you would be you telling them to get out, then you have answered your own question.

On the other hand, the positive movement forward can bring hope.

This positive side to hope brings you to freedom through the courage of doing what's right for you.

The Positive Emotional Response, when done correctly, brings deep personal inner strength.

This is for your soul and your well-being so do what makes you happy.

If you can find the slightest strength within yourself then there is hope.

Remember hope brings us out of the darkness and into the light.

It can break the chains that bind you to the loneliness you feel and bring you into the blissful feeling of empowerment!

With this new empowerment you can dig your way out of the entrapment of your previously lonely and loveless lifestyle.

The reason I believe it's one of the hardest forms of loneliness is because there is nothing worse than being with someone and feeling totally alone.

But remember if you're enduring it that means you have strength to get out of it.

So, it's time to harness that strength so we can build ourselves up again and finally wield your ax and cut the chains that bind us!

Only you can do it.

I don't want you to die alone in a relationship that makes you feel that way.

So, it's time to walk off the path of loneliness and go from the loneliness journey to the freedom journey.

Now fair warning, this journey will be lonely at first, but it will be liberating in due time.

Once you find faith in yourself you will be able to find the faith in others and remember what love is all about.

Until then you will be right there with the people you feel close to.

Remember in this loneliest journey you're never truly alone.

The third type of single person is someone on the search for a meaningful relationship.

This type of single person is typically someone who is in the dating game and who is going out very often to cope with the isolation of being single.

They choose to date and socialize with people just so they can have the company of another physical person, even if it is just for one evening.

But this doesn't mean they don't feel alone.

They justify this companionship as not being alone, but when they go home, they're still very lonely.

Searching brings us to dating sites or dating apps, to mindlessly going out just to find someone to fill a void.

They gather at different social events just so they can look for someone there to fill this empty space inside.

This type of interaction can be very important to fill the gap in our lives or it might lead to settling for what we can get in order not to be lonely.

But the truth of the matter is, this coping mechanism can make for an overall destructive experience.

We will usually be met with disappointment or regret.

It's okay to go through this behavior short-term, because it is part of the journey and path that you're on.

Plus, it can be part of the process of self-improvement.

It can also lead to an understanding of what this brokenness is and how it feels to be in that state of mind.

What counts is that we're growing in these moments and becoming better from them.

We can understand that we're not alone through faith, belief, hope, and encouragement.

So, no matter what pain you've been through, tears will dry, broken hearts will heal, and somewhere a person who truly cares is waiting for you.

"If you focus on the hurt, you will continue to suffer. If you focus on the lesson you will continue to grow"

Which I will talk about greatly in the next few chapters.

Just remember you're not alone within your pain.

"Lonely hearts with lonely days, enter darken pathways. But if we can just hold on a little longer, we can find solutions to enter into the light of unbroken days to fulfill our ways. The path will seem so clear in the inner vision of the battlefields that later on will calm our pond".

NOTES

NOTES

Chapter Seven

WALKING AMONG BROKEN PIECES

---

*"I finally understand that
people hurt me because of
where they are in their own
lives; they are expressing
their brokenness-not my
worth" Unknown*

THE QUOTE ABOVE holds so much truth especially for those of us entering a relationship where the brokenness is evident from the start.

Now, we might be walking in with our own broken state.

The question then becomes, do I want to still walk among those broken pieces?

The choice we are then faced with is very real.

Do we rough it out and go through the brokenness with them, or do we leave?

Remember, you'll have to walk along with them in their brokenness.

This is a crucial decision that must be taken before we continue down this path.

We don't want to create more brokenness for someone else if we don't have to.

This is where we need to step back and reflect on where we are in our own lives.

It is time to take a closer look into our mental state.

We should monitor out internal dialogue, for example.

Do we still make negative emotional reactions and responses?

Are we even still broken?

How much strength and positive emotional energy do you have available to support someone else's broken pieces?

This won't be easy for either of you.

But you will have to take the decision.

That's why your process for assessing your internal dialogue and self-reflection has to be honest, concise, and certain in these moments.

Your life isn't the only one that will be impacted if the wrong decision is made.

Multiple lives can be affected, especially if your partner has children.

Remember, someone's brokenness can bleed into other loved ones who have been around it.

So, in this instance, we should be very careful and step cautiously when acting on our decision, if we are lucky enough to recognize the inner brokenness of the other person.

Remember, sometimes the other individual will mask their broken pieces so well that we could miss the signs completely for days, months, or even years, while we are walking along with them.

People can carry these broken pieces with them for so long that they become a part of them, to the extent that these broken pieces and negative emotional responses have become part of their daily routine - even if they aren't aware of them.

It's been my personal experience that not everyone will share his or her brokenness with you.

So, we need to really listen to the words and responses of the other person to help us see where they are in their lives and to understand and recognize their thought patterns.

This will help us with making the decision as to whether are not we're willing to walk down their path alongside them.

Through learning the other person's responses, you will learn how to properly react.

You never stop learning about your partner.

When you reach the level of understanding where they feel safe enough to reveal aspects of the closed paths, the curtain covering those negative experiences and situations will be pulled back, to reveal the deep oceans and dark pathways that have informed their belief systems and behavior patterns.

Only time will allow this to happen.

Your partner needs to feel safe. They will be trusting you with truths that make them feel at their most vulnerable.

Do we want to rescue them up from above the dark cold ocean so they can breathe and come alive in the fresh air?

Do we want to walk by their side down the dark pathway of their brokenness to help your partner step into the light?

You will become the tide that brings the water to the shore, even if we have to go beneath the surface of the water in order to arise up again.

To become the light in the dark pathway on someone else's journey, we need to become his or her shadow.

To seek light, you must first step into the darkness.

Stumbling into Brokenness

When you stumble into someone else's brokenness, you might be not even aware of their internal negative state. Things are rarely as they appear on the surface.

Here is the scenario: You meet someone special that you feel a strong connection with at first.

When you meet that person, they may be putting their best foot forward and representing the best version of themselves that they are capable of being at that time.

Then, as time goes on, you start noticing subtle changes in their behavior or even worse you might not notice any changes at all.

But due to the sheer nature of your connectivity, you might think it's your own mind or heart playing tricks on you.

This is what it means to walk among broken pieces, and it is simply not possible to do this when you yourself are still broken.

We just have to remember that by being there through someone's brokenness, we are most likely able to heal our own brokenness by understanding that we aren't alone and that our personal negative thinking and responses may not be as bad as we had believed or imagined.

"You never truly know how damaged a person is until you try to love them."

Unknown

NOTES

NOTES

_____

_____

_____

_____

_____

_____

_____

_____

_____

_____

_____

_____

_____

"When one door of happiness closes, another opens; but often we look so long at the closed door that we do not see the one which has been opened for us."

Helen Keller

Chapter Eight

CLOSURE MOMENTS

THE WAY TO CLOSURE is to leave behind any anger, resentment, and sadness from past events, experiences and situations.

Getting closure is a very important part of the rebuilding and restoration process.

Making amends for your negative past behaviors and emotional responses will help you find peace whether it is with ourselves or the other person that left us.

We have to find this peace in order to move on and move forward, otherwise we will get lost within the feelings of regret and hang on to them.

We have to let go of the negative emotional responses of past experiences.

Now I understand why we hold onto these emotions; it is because we're not ready to move on.

This could be due to fear or loss, but I believe it's because the emotional connections we make with the other person during the relationship.

Think about it. When a loved one dies, we have a viewing or ceremonial funeral.

It helps us find closure in someone's death.

We usually don't find closure if we don't know how they died.

Hence, a medical autopsy is performed when a death as occurred. They're performed to help the loved ones with closure through the act of knowing the facts behind the death.

Now, a shift happens when the heartache strikes when someone still living leaves us.

We wonder why they left and when we can't find these answers, we search for them.

This when we start becoming a private investigator, searching high and low for answers and explanations as to why we were rejected and left alone.

We find it hard to continue to move forward especially if there is no closure to why they got up and left in the first place.

If we know why they left, either due to deceit, betrayal, and by a lack of loyalty, we still want closure from that experience before we can let our heart go on.

If we don't get it, then naturally we will make our own reasons and explanations, imaginary or otherwise.

Sometimes we're not left with any other choice but to do this in order to move on.

Now I know this feels useless, but it's a necessary part of moving on.

NOTES

NOTES

Chapter Nine

CREATING A BETTER PATH

CLOSURE SETS US IN THE DIRECTION of creating a better and brighter path, full of positive energy.

Once we find closure, then the path that we're on becomes clearer. We can see the light at the end of the road which is bright with visions of hope.

We have a sense of life again.

Where we once felt that our life was over, due to the pain and sorrow our heartfelt at that time, we can start becoming reborn in the moment of our enlightenment.

You can start over at any point in your life. You can start over with someone that you're currently with or start over with someone new.

If we decide that we are going to make it work with the person that we want to stay with, I suggest that we take some additional measures such as counseling sessions to help understand each other.

It can help to have a third-party mediator when the pain is too hard to handle on our own.

Sometimes it's not enough to want to be right.

We have to be aware of this, if we want to make it work with the other person and build a solid foundation for our improved relationship.

This is where we should drop our defensive position in an argument and just surrender to moving on with our lives in a more positive way.

Compromises should be made to help the relationship regain its momentum. It's all about reconnecting and finding the spark that has been lost.

Losing hope isn't an option when you go down this path.

Stay strong in your efforts and stay on the track. But you have to remember that you both have to get to know each other all over again.

Yes, it is possible that it can happen for two people to regain their passion.

But both of you have to want it and be willing to do the work and commit to it.

Sometimes it doesn't work, but we still have to be willing to open up our heart to be able to reconnect with anyone.

For some, this might be challenging but it is achievable.

Just open up the forgiveness portal that's in your heart and you will see just what I'm talking about.

We won't allow our heart to move on due to the three Fs that trap us in past experiences.

FEAR can stop us from being able to move on.

Fear can be so toxic to the developmental stages of improvement that we can become frozen in any attempts to move forward.

This fear is always occupied by the same questions that we all hear or say to ourselves;

- What if it doesn't work?

- What if I am rejected again?

- How can I come back from this?

These questions should be replaced with;

- What will I do when it does work?

- How will I feel?

- How will I act and think differently?

This leads back to the positive emotional response that we will hold and carry through this developmental stage.

FORGETTING is hard to do.

Now I'm not saying you're going to forget about those negative emotional experiences, because that won't happen.

What I am saying is that forgetting to let go of those negative experiences can stop you from moving on.

You have to let go of the negative emotional responses associated with those experiences and situations.

By letting go, you're not tied down and shackled to them anymore.

You are free to build and restore broken relationships.

FORGIVENESS.

We have to forgive ourselves first, as I explained before.

This step is just as important as the first two.

It liberates us and really gives us a chance to reopen the door to our heart that we once closed shut.

Some of you might be asking yourselves, "how do I do this?"

The answer can be explained in a single word.

SURRENDERING

Surrendering is most likely not the answer you were expecting. It is such a difficult thing to do when your mind won't clear.

It is part of forgiveness.

This kind of surrendering is not your typical surrendering where you hold up a white flag.

This surrendering is about giving in, not giving up.

This surrendering gives us the room to let someone else in, but what it does more than that is open us up to ourselves again.

When we think about relationships on a soulful and emotional level, we usually always leave ourselves out of it.

We can't and shouldn't forget about ourselves.

This is so important and yet so often we forget about self-care and self-love.

We're a fundamental part of this equation more than the other soul is, believe it are not.

Now I know this might seem selfish at first glance, but if you take a closer look, you'll see it's not.

It's not selfish to believe that you are the most important person in your life. It is quite true that no one is going to love yourself more than you will.

We have to be okay with surrendering ourselves to ourselves so that we can love ourselves the way we're meant too.

Only then can we fill the void with another soul and go into any relationship with a solid foundation of self-belief and self-awareness.

We have to be comfortable in knowing that we are the most important person in our lives.

Only then can we completely be ready to move on.

It starts with us and ends with everyone else.

Without surrendering to our own needs first, we can't give the best part of ourselves to the other people in our lives.

This leads us into creating a better path for our lives and the lives of those we care about.

SURRENDERING OF GUILT

This type of surrendering is also very important for the ones that have lost a loved one to either suicide or a tragic event that was unpreventable.

These losses include those from car accidents, war, an unpreventable health problem or a mysterious unknown death.

You can walk in this guilt for the rest of your days if you don't surrender and understand you couldn't do anything to change the tragic outcome.

We all have to understand that this type of surrendering is not giving up your power.

You're giving yourself the courage to realize that this guilt doesn't have to hold you to the negativity we feel in our hearts.

This surrender of guilt is a release of heartache.

This doesn't mean you have to let go of the memory of that loved one; it just means you're giving into your power of forgiveness and acceptance again.

Once you accept that it wasn't your fault, you then can seek resolution within you mind, heart, and soul.

This creates a better path for us to move on and forward.

By surrendering, we learn to let go of the guilt that has been haunting us and making us feel as though we shouldn't be the ones left behind.

This gives us a chance to create a reason to be here and also realize that our loved ones would want something better for us.

It's all about creating a better path for a better future.

If you've been brutally broken but you still have the courage to be gentle to other living beings, then you're a badass with a heart of an angel.

Keanu Reeves

NOTES

Chapter Ten

UNBROKEN ROADS TO REDEMPTION

ONCE WE HAVE STEPPED ONTO A BETTER PATH, we can finally walk on unbroken roads towards redemption and becoming the best possible version of ourselves.

Life doesn't have to be so broken.

Once we realize that we can take steps to understand and mend the broken paths that we have walked on in the past, it suddenly becomes clear that we don't have to stay on those paths!

Redemption is the process of knowing what to do and how to respond to the hardships that we all go through.

I want you to find redemption for yourself, your loved ones that have passed, and the ones that are still here with you today.

You *deserve* the best that life has to offer.

You *deserve* to have the opportunity to realize your potential and enjoy the lifestyle that you have been searching for.

I know from my own experiences what it feels like to break free of negative emotional responses and to move forward with positive energy and hope.

My own story makes this apparent.

I came from a broken home but was saved when I was seven years old. Now I could have lived in this brokenness for the rest of my days, but I chose not to, for the sake of the people I have the privilege of calling mom and dad.

They taught me how to forgive at a young age, but I didn't quite understand the true power of that lesson until I was older.

When my marriage failed, I finally realized the extreme power of being able to forgive and move forward onto a positive path.

My ex-wife and I have such a wonderful relationship now because of this power, which some people find it odd to say the least.

It makes it more amazing because our kids can be freely involved with her step kids. They get to see the transformational power of self-belief and positive emotional responses, which is one of the greatest benefits about this healing process.

My ex-wife's new husband is also a contributing factor in this.

We all have such an amazing relationship for the kids and ourselves, that when my ex-wife's partner proposed to her, they both called me to let me know that they were getting married.

That's when they both invited me to their wedding.

I know most of you are probably thinking that I didn't go.

Well I did go, because even though my marriage did not work out, I only want my ex-wife to be happy.

If she couldn't be happy with me, then why wouldn't I want to see her happy with someone else? Our relationship can still be special and caring but in a different way.

This is the amazing power of being unbroken on my own road to redemption.

This is all due to the way I respond to any negative experiences I have been through.

I controlled those moments by responding in the way that would bring the most positive benefits to my life and the people in my life who I care about.

We can all become broken through heartache, disappointment, sadness, unfulfilled promises, and also through anger, hatred, bitterness, loss, and the unwavering thought of never being able to forgive ourselves.

Letting go of these powerful negative emotional responses and giving your all to the process of moving forwards in a positive way is the best way to living a life walked on unbroken paths and regaining control of your life again.

We can move forward through any experiences we go through in life and find the mended road to redemption.

I know that understanding and mending my own brokenness has allowed me to better serve others and to pass my knowledge to everyone I come into contact with.

So here is to your journey!

May it be a life of understanding and mending.

Through trials, triumphs, and tribulations the path you currently walk on doesn't have to be broken.

A healthy and happy better path awaits you and everyone you love.

Remember better days can be seen beyond the pain of any negative emotional response that you have been through. Walk towards the light and come out of the broken darkness you feel inside.

If I can do it so can you.

Have faith, love, and happiness guide you to this better path.

THANK YOU

I want to thank you for taking the time for reading this book.

It is my profound hope that it has helped you along your broken path and you are finally able to discover a path to redemption for yourself.

Sometimes the bad things that happen in our lives put us directly on the path to the best things that will ever happen to us.

ABOUT THE AUTHOR

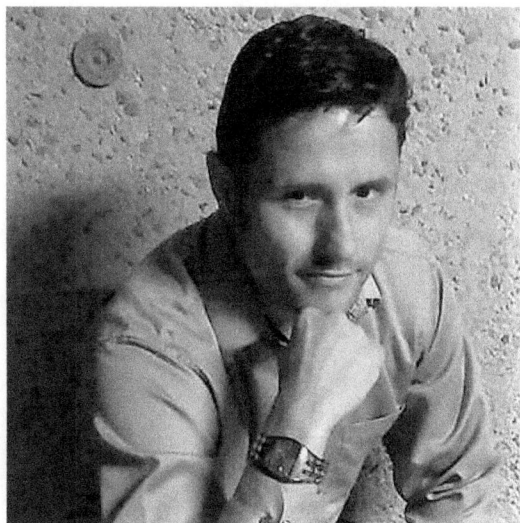

Sean Alexander Hamilton is passionate about changing the course of people's lives through his writing and coaching services.

Through a deep understanding of the human condition, Sean is an expert in building and restoring relationships.

His goal is to provide tools, ideas, and thought-provoking concepts to change the lives of his readers, clients and everyone he encounters.

Find out more at:
ww.alexanderhamiltonsinsights.com

www.alexanderhamiltonsinsights.com

www.ingramcontent.com/pod-product-compliance
Lightning Source LLC
La Vergne TN
LVHW021507080426
835509LV00018B/2422